C000187016

MUNSTER
Heineken Cup 2008
Champions of Europe

MUNSTER
Heineken Cup 2008
Champions of Europe

Photographs by **Inpho Photography**

Contemporaneous Match Reports from the **Irish Examiner**

Gill & Macmillan Ltd
Hume Avenue, Park West, Dublin 12
with associated companies throughout the world
www.gillmacmillan.ie

© Introduction and arrangement of material, Munster Branch IRFU 2008
© Photographs, Inpho Photography 2008
© Match Reports, Irish Examiner 2008

978 07171 4597 3

Book design and typesetting by Design Image, Dublin
Printed and bound in Italy by L.E.G.O. SpA

This book is typeset in Janson 9pt on 13pt.

The paper used in this book comes from the wood pulp of managed forests.
For every tree felled, at least one tree is planted, thereby renewing natural resources.

A CIP catalogue record for this book is available from the British Library.

1 3 5 4 2

Contents

OFFICERS 2008

Gerry O'Loughlin	President
Nicholas Comyn	Vice President
Declan Madden	Junior Vice President
Frank Byford	Hon. Secretary
Jim Riordan	Hon. Treasurer

STAFF 2008

Garrett Fitzgerald	Chief Executive
Ultan O'Callaghan	Provincial Domestic Games Manager
Philip Quinn	Finance Manager
Glyn Billinghurst	Sales and Marketing Manager
Claire Cooke	HR Manager and Brand Compliance
Trish Drinan	Event Manager and PR Domestic Game
Jennifer Kiernan	Supporters Club Manager
Karen Lewis	Ticket Office Manager
Fiona Murphy	E-Commerce Executive
John Coleman	Branch Administrator
Frances Bowen	Accounts Assistant
Teresa McCullagh	Accounts Assistant
Jessica Foran	Ticket & Supporters Club Admin. Assistant
Gerry Moore	Assistant Branch Administrator
Judi Kennedy	Admin. Assistant / Receptionist - Limerick
Claire Hickey	Admin. Assistant / Receptionist – Cork
Damon Urlich	Club Development Manager
Catherine Carroll	Provincial Programmes Manager
Gemma Crowley	Women's Regional Development Officer
Cliona Quaid	Development Office Administrator
Tom Holbrook	Musgrave Park Groundsman
Liam McCarthy	Thomond Park Groundsman
John Lacey	Regional Development Officer
Finny O'Regan	Regional Development Officer
John O'Neill	Regional Development Officer
Paul Collins	Regional Development Officer

Hamish Adams	Academy Manager (outgoing)
Ian Sherwin	Academy Manager (incoming)
Ken O'Connell	Elite Rugby Development Officer
Paudie Roche	Sub Academy Fitness Coach – Cork
Ray Egan	Sub Academy Fitness Coach – Limerick
All Youth Development Officers	

The Full Team

SQUAD

Federico Pucciariello	Prop		Alan Quinlan	Back row
Tony Buckley	Prop		Jake Paringatai	Back row
Darragh Hurley	Prop		Frank Sheahan	Hooker
Jerry Flannery	Hooker		Niall Ronan	Back row
Anthony Foley	Back row		Peter Stringer	Scrum Half
John O'Sullivan	Back row		Shaun Payne	Full Back
John Hayes	Prop		David Wallace	Back row
Mick O'Driscoll	Lock		Ian Dowling	Wing
Marcus Horan	Prop		Barry Murphy	Centre
Anthony Horgan	Wing		Kieran Lewis	Centre
Donnacha Ryan	Lock		Brian Carney	Wing
John Kelly	Centre		Lifeimi Mafi	Centre
Paul O'Connell	Lock		Paul Warwick	Outhalf
Eugene McGovern	Prop		James Coughlan	Back row
Denis Fogarty	Hooker		Rua Tipoki	Centre
Tomás O'Leary	Scrum Half		Denis Hurley	Full Back
Doug Howlett	Wing		Tim Ryan	Prop
Donncha O'Callaghan	Lock		Tom Gleeson	Centre
Jeremy Manning	Outhalf		Ciaran O'Boyle	Wing
Ronan O'Gara	Outhalf		Mark Melbourne	Lock
Mossie Lawler	Wing		Keith Earls	Wing
Denis Leamy	Back row		Gerry Hurley	Scrum Half

MANAGEMENT

Declan Kidney	Director of Coaching		Fergal O'Callaghan	Conditioning Coach
Jerry Holland	Team Manager		Aidan O'Connell	Conditioning Coach
Tony McGahan	Backs/Defensive Coach		Tom Comyns	Conditioning Coach
Jim Williams	Forwards Coach		Anthony Coole	Physiotherapist
Paul McCarthy	Specialist Coach - Scrum		John Casey	Physiotherapist
Mark Tainton	Specialist Coach - Kicking		Dave Revins	Masseur
Jason Holland	Video Analyst		Martin McPhail	Masseur
Bryan Murphy	Operations Manager		Jack Kiely	Kit Manager
Pat Geraghty	Media Manager		Ian Fleming	Equipment Manager
Tadgh O'Sullivan	Doctor		Martin Joyce	Kit Assistant 1
Mick Shinkwin	Doctor		Ian Dunne	Kit Assistant 2
Declan Aherne	Team Psychologist		Andrea Cullen	Nutritionist
Paul Darbyshire	Head of Conditioning			

Then where does
the power come from,
to see the race to its end?

From within.

Chariots of Fire

Introduction

Michael Moynihan

Then where does the power come from, to see the race to its end? From within.

IT seems appropriate to kick off with the above quote from Chariots of Fire, because it expresses a couple of imperishable truths about Munster's latest Heineken Cup victory. One relates to the spirit necessary to drive on to the summit, something this Munster team has never lacked.

The second thought that occurs is that a chariot, fiery or otherwise, is probably the only mode of transport that Munster fans have yet to adopt in order to get to a big game.

It's different this time. It has to be. The relief that was visible in 2006 was born of heartbreak, of having been so close to victory in the past that you could touch its sleeve as it passed by, like a stranger in the crowd. When Peter Stringer booted that last ball into the second tier of the Millennium Stadium at the final whistle against Biarritz, he was doing more than killing the game. He was kicking away the bad memories.

It was different this time. There were different challenges to confront, and throughout the season, of all the teams involved, Munster were the best equipped to handle them. All through the season they've shown the benefits of experience, a woolly word that never seems to be fully defined in the past, though there are plenty of examples to choose from after this last twelve months.

Having been there before was never so valuable. Munster could raid the memory bank any time they faced adversity, and they knew they could survive. Trailing Clermont Auvergne by seventeen points in France would have been a suffocating pressure for many teams, but Munster's calmness told. Recalling some other brutal away days helped when facing Gloucester in front of the Shed, a prospect which has paralysed many a highly-regarded Premiership outfit. Dealing with a Saracens team only too happy to drape themselves in the underdog's colours was a different challenge. That, too, was a hurdle negotiated; dealing with the race from the favourite's lane, not just the outsider's, is what separates a champion from all the rest. In the final itself, during that last discussion between O'Gara and O'Connell about the late, late penalty, the out-half had the experience to ask what would happen if he kicked for the posts and his shot rebounded, and Toulouse counterattacked . . .

They say you can't buy experience; you couldn't even bid for that kind of nous.

It's strange to view the final itself again now. The last steps to the summit always look inevitable and as the dying seconds of the final itself against Toulouse tick away on the VT, the victory looks inevitable; to shake the rust off an old cliché, it looks as though Munster's name was on the trophy.

It was anything but. Just to give everything a little context, think back a few months. In late September, Munster welcomed their World Cup players back from France. Paul O'Connell was a long-term injury, new signing Doug Howlett wouldn't be available until after Christmas, and there was no shortage of suggestions that Munster's interest in the European competition mightn't even be more than academic at that stage.

That was understandable, given the company in their pool. Wasps, who defeated Munster in the seismic 2004 semi-final; Clermont Auvergne, the free-spending French powerhouse who'd snapped up World Cup-winning captain John Smit; and Llanelli, who'd knocked Munster out in the 2007 quarter-final.

If not a Group of Death, then surely a Group of "Life Flashing Before Your Eyes Before You Move Towards The Light".

And yet. And yet. By November Munster had collected an invaluable moral victory away to Wasps, losing narrowly. For a team which deals in the hard currency of real wins that might sound a backhanded compliment, but losing to Wasps by just a point was a fair return, particularly when Munster had led by ten points at one stage in the second half. The simple fact that Ronan O'Gara was back on form was a huge boost.

From there the team built. We take their experience for granted, but doing the right thing is never as obvious as you think. For an obvious comparison, think back to November, when Clermont Auvergne gambled hugely resting several front line players for their trip to Thomond Park.

The fact that Munster – both team and supporters – take umbrage at any slight, real or imagined, must be one of the worst-kept secrets

Munster players at the launc
of the new kit

Peter Stringer getting the ball away

in world sport at this stage, so what was Clermont coach Vern Cotter thinking? The French outfit clearly felt a formidable record at the Stade Marcel Michelin would help them to gather the bonus points necessary to qualify for the knock-out stages, but after the implied insult sank in – no matter what happens in Limerick, we'll remedy it at home – the apparent disregard only sharpened the appetite. Munster duly accepted the bonus point win in Limerick.

There was another fillip before Christmas, when Munster had too much for Llanelli in Wales. The game has gone down in history for the 31 phases in which Munster kept possession but the performance was another marker. That 2007 quarter-final was avenged, a key to the driving control shown by the forwards under the leadership of Anthony Foley, that hero of a thousand battles, and O'Gara's seven-from-seven with the boot confirmed the return to form.

After that it was time to introduce Clermont to the realities of the Heineken Cup. Munster fell behind in the second half and looked to be out of it, but they rallied to work the ball from somewhere near Paris to the Clermont try-line, Lifeimi Mafi touching down for the vital score. Another defeat, but another bonus point.

There were other games to come, including a fine win over Wasps crowned by Denis Leamy's try, and if anyone doubted Munster's ability to gather their lessons on the hoof, consider Laurence Dallaglio's complaints – delivered with a straight face – about the referee after Wasps were comprehensively beaten in Thomond Park. The great English forward spent much of his career deafening referees himself; his implicit admission of lack of influence was a backhanded compliment to Munster's ability to handle everything thrown up on the field of play.

DALLAGLIO
CORAL.co.uk
8

O'Gara sees the funny side

So where does the power come from? Throughout the campaign at various stages, different players stepped up to the mark. Throughout the campaign questions were asked of this Munster squad and the answers were clear and unequivocal. In the defeat or victory there is no discernible difference in how the Munster players or their coaches conduct themselves and it was noticeable how they sought out the opposition in the Millennium Stadium after the initial euphoria of victory had washed over. Even at the very end Munster knew how to behave. It was plain that as the teams milled around before the presentation of the trophy that Donncha O'Callaghan was seeking Fabien Pelous to shake his hand. Declan Kidney's route to join his squad took in each of the disconsolate French players standing to the left of the podium.

A quiet word, a gentle handshake.

It's all different now. As happens to all teams, people move on. In the immediate aftermath of the win there were no retirements announced by players, sated by their second European Cup. Much of the change came off-stage.

Declan Kidney takes charge of the national Squad, a just reward for a great coach. Anthony Foley, John Foley and Mossy Lawler have finished up. So too Eugene McGovern and Gerry Hurley. So a link with the barnstorming All-Ireland League days is gone. Shaun Payne moves upstairs and Jim Williams who arrived as a stranger returns to Australia as a red icon.

Introduction

United we stand

10 November 2007

Match 1

London Wasps 24 – 23 Munster
The Ricoh Arena

Edged out by a single point

Match report, 12 November 2007

LONDON WASPS edged out Munster by a single point, in a hugely-entertaining and full-blooded contest and having come from 10 points behind in either half, just about deserved to do so.

The sad fact, however, is that at least one of these two outstanding sides will be out of the competition in mid-January.

Indeed, a similar fate awaits Llanelli Scarlets and Clermont-Auvergne, the two other smashing sides in the same pool.

The clash of Wasps and Munster was light years ahead of much of what we witnessed at the World Cup, but that's for another day.

Already, Munster are gathering themselves for another massive engagement against the money machine that is Clermont Auvergne at Thomond Park on Sunday next. They recognise that another defeat – in spite of Saturday's welcome bonus point – could to all intents and purposes end their hopes of emerging from this pool.

There were so many turning points in front of the 21,506 fans at the Ricoh that it is difficult to programme them all. Munster fans will point to the key moments when it looked as if Brian Carney was flagrantly obstructed by Fraser Waters just after half

time with a try a near certainty and when Marcus Horan was yellow carded for preventing clean possession when he and numerous others in the Ricoh believed the ball was out and he was perfectly entitled to make his move.

That said, referee Malcolm Changleng's decision to rule as forward the pass from Paul Sackey to Danny Cipriani that deprived Wasps of a first half try was marginal while the TMO had good reason to take his time before deciding that Peter Stringer with the help of David Wallace had prevented Sackey from making a fair touch down when many read the situation otherwise. So – let's not blame the ref.

Munster now have a long road to travel if they are to reach the knock-out stages for the 10th successive year. They must win their home matches starting with the French on Sunday. But the signs are positive in spite of this single point loss.

Ronan O'Gara's wellbeing was a joy to

LONDON WASPS:

M Van Gisbergen
P Sackey
F Waters
R Flutey
T Voyce
D Cipriani
E Reddan
T Payne
R Ibañez
N Adams
S Shaw
G Skivington
J Haskell
T Rees
L Dallaglio (capt)

Replacements:
J Hart for (Dallaglio 53 min)
M Holford (Payne 65 min)
J Ward (Adams 72 min)
D Leo (Holford 79 min)
R Birkett
S Amor
R Hoadley

MUNSTER:

S Payne
B Carney
L Mafi
R Tipoki
A Horgan
R O'Gara (capt)
P Stringer
M Horan
J Flannery
J Hayes
D O'Callaghan
M O'Driscoll
A Quinlan
D Wallace
D Leamy

Replacements:
F Sheahan
T Buckley (Hayes 37 min)
A Foley (Buckley 77 min)
J Parimgatai (Horan 77 min)
T O'Leary (Payne 75 min)
P Warwick
K Lewis

Referee:
M Changleng (Scotland)

SCORING   1st Half   **5 mins:** O'Gara pen 0-3; **8 mins:** Cipriani pen 3-3; **17 mins:** O'Gara pen 3-6; **20 mins:** Tipoki try, O'Gara con 3-13; **30 mins:** Cipriani pen 6-13; **31mins:** Flutey try, Cipriani con 13-13; **40 mins (+4):** Payne try, O'Gara con 13-20
Half Time 13-20
2nd Half   **44 mins:** O'Gara pen 13-23; **53 mins:** Cipriani pen 16-23; **57 mins:** Cipriani pen 19-23; **60 mins:** Skivington try 24-23
Full Time 24-23

A questioning Ronan O'Gara

behold and it was manifestly evident why he delighted in playing alongside the New Zealand midfield axis of Rua Tipoki and Lifeimi Mafi. The try the Kiwis conjured between them was of the highest quality and O'Gara's sublime little chip through for Shaun Payne's try left us grappling for superlatives. When Rog is in this kind of form, there is always reason for hope.

However there were several grey areas, with the manner in which they dealt with the restart a particular problem. As the game went on, one sensed Wasps would gain possession from the kick-off and they invariably did so, more often than not imposing fierce pressure on Munster in the process. The line-out worked well with Mick O'Driscoll and Donncha O'Callaghan pinching a few Wasps darts while comfortable enough on their own throw.

Declan Kidney will also examine the concession of a few needless and crucial penalties.

There was also the occasion when, having withstood intense pressure for a lengthy spell in their own 22, Munster somehow turned over possession and looked to have every chance of scoring at the other end only to squander that opportunity with a sliced kick into touch.

Anthony Foley and Tomás O'Leary about to join the fray

Van Gisbergen under pressure

O'Gara chips ahead

Lifeimi Mafi congratulated by his team mates

Match 2

Munster 36 – 13 ASM Clermont Auvergne
Thomond Park

Battling Munster bag vital bonus point

Match report, 19 November 2007

FIVE tries, four of them deliciously created, produced the all-important bonus point for Munster in the somewhat surreal surroundings of Thomond Park yesterday.

There is still a long, hard road to travel in Pool 5 of the Heineken Cup and coach Declan Kidney readily accepts that there are several areas of the side where considerable improvement is essential.

Clermont Auvergne picked a strange team yesterday, but they were never going to do a Bourgoin on it. They competed for everything and it was only in the final ten minutes that the fourth try was conceded. They were even thinking there might be something in the game for themselves, until that late surge brought tries for Alan Quinlan and Marcus Horan.

A 17-6 half time lead was priceless from a Munster viewpoint and justified the home side's decision to hand the visitors the wind, having won the toss. It could have been more, considering their failure to score while Vilomoni Delasau was in the bin having been harshly dismissed as early as the tenth minute for killing the ball illegally at a ruck near his own line.

Quick as a flash, O'Gara realised that the right wing side was totally undefended and placed a pinpoint kick in the path of Lifeimi Mafi and Shaun Payne. The former allowed the ball to run through to Payne, who had a simple task in scoring. O'Gara converted and Munster were on their way.

Clermont quickly narrowed the gap with a penalty by out-half Seremia Bai. Munster retained the initiative, but failed to capitalise on the extra man and Delasau had returned to the action when O'Gara knocked over a penalty on 37 minutes to put his side 10-3 in front. However, from the kick-off, which was safely gathered by Mick O'Driscoll, Munster were penalised for crossing – a decision that baffled most of the attendance – and Bai knocked over his second goal.

However, the half ended as the fans would have wished: Alan Quinlan charged down an attempted Bai clearance, only to have the ball dashed from his grasp as he dived to score. Clermont managed to clear to touch,

MUNSTER:
S Payne
B Carney
L Mafi
R Tipoki
I Dowling
R O'Gara (capt)
P Stringer
M Horan
J Flannery
J Hayes
D O'Callaghan
M O'Driscoll
A Quinlan
D Wallace
D Leamy

Replacements:
F Sheahan (Flannery 78 min)
T Buckley (Hayes 63 min)
A Foley (Wallace 69 min)
J Paringatai (Quinlan 78 min)
G Hurley (Stringer 78 min)
P Warwick (O'Gara 78min)
K Lewis (Tipoki 78min)

ASM CLERMONT AUVERGNE:
J Malzieu
G Esterhuizen
M Joubert
R Chanal
V Delasau
S Bai
A Pic
G Shvelidze
J Smit
D Zirakashvili
C Samson
P Vigouroux
F Alexandre
E Etien
S Broomhall (capt)

Replacements:
T Domingo (Shvelidze 45 min)
T Privat (Vigouroux 46 min)
A Audfebart (Etien 50 min)
M Lozupone (Smit 55-58min & 63-67 min)
P Manuel Garcia (Chanal 60 min)
N Vonowale Nalaga (Joubert 74 min)
A King

Referee:
N Owens (Wales)

SCORING

1st Half
7 mins: Payne try, O'Gara con, 7-0; **11 mins:** Bai penalty, 7-3;
36 mins: O'Gara pen 10-3; **38 mins:** Bai penalty, 10-6; **40 mins:** Tipoki try, O'Gara con, 17-6
Half Time 17-6

2nd Half
51 mins: Carney try, O'Gara con, 24-6; **63 mins:** Joubert try, Bai con, 24-13;
76 mins: Quinlan try, O'Gara con, 31-13; **79 mins:** Horan try, 36-13
Full Time 36-13

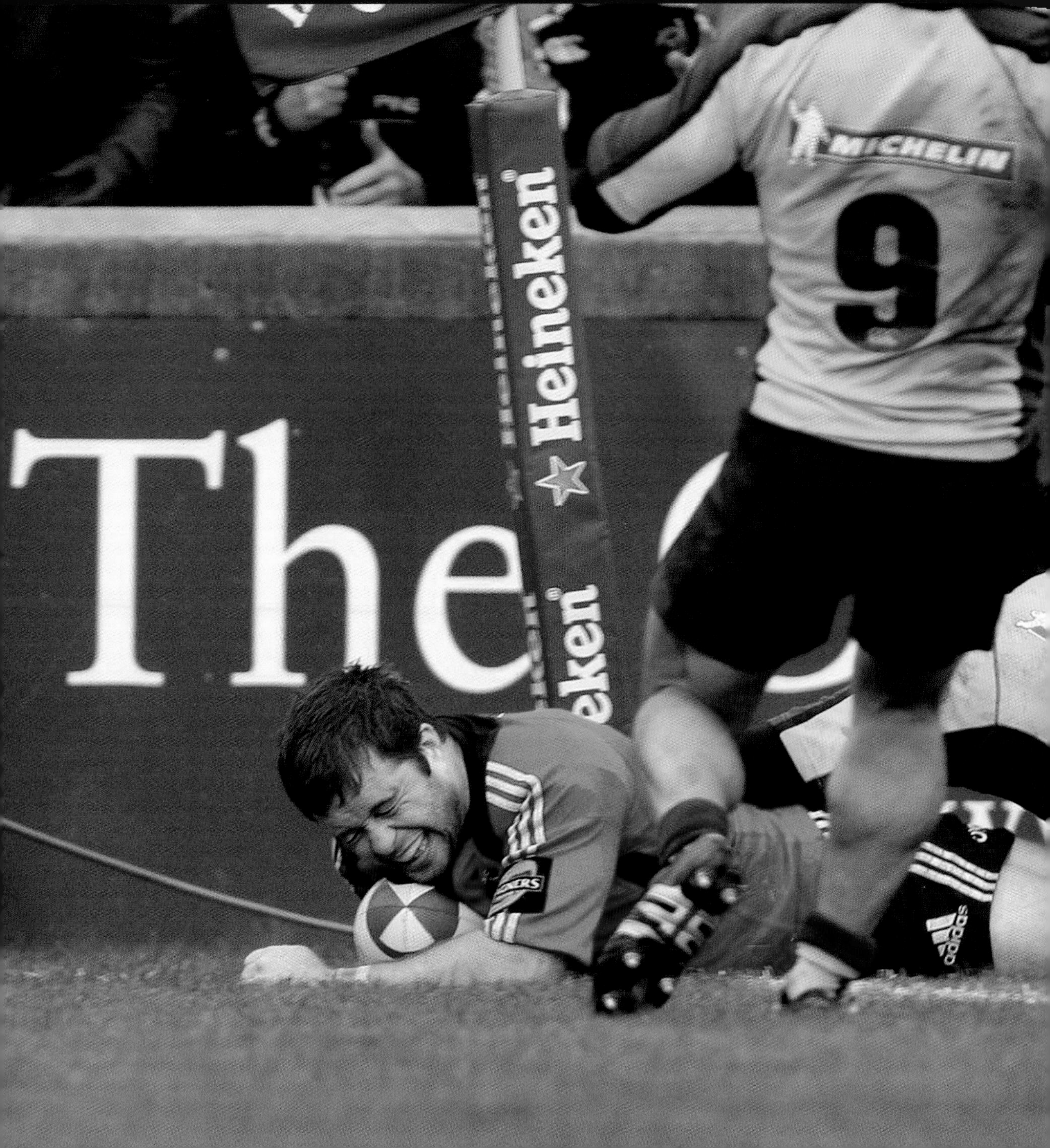

MICHELIN
9
Heineken
Heineken
The

but Munster rolled the ensuing line-out and having been momentarily held up, got the ball to Rua Tipoki who brushed past the attempted tackle of Emmanuel Etian to get the touchdown. O'Gara added the points with a fine kick and Munster were looking good.

Ten minutes into the second half, the outcome of the game was assured.

After consistent pressure, Munster attacked off a set scrum and O'Gara linked with Payne, who judged his overhead pass to perfection to send Brian Carney in unopposed. O'Gara converted to make it 24-6 and now it was a case of claiming the all important fourth try.

First, though, they had to handle a Clermont side now beginning to believe more and more in itself. That was certainly the case when former Springbok centre Marius Joubert charged down Tipoki's clearing kick on 65 minutes and easily got the touchdown for a try that Bai converted.

The bonus finally came Munster's way in the 76th minute when, courtesy of a succession of Clermont defensive errors, Quinlan was deemed by the television match official Derek Bevan to have got the touchdown. O'Gara knocked over the conversion and the fifth try duly came again from Marcus Horan after another superb overhead pass, this time by Denis Leamy.

Marcus Horan scores the fifth try

15

Mick O'Driscoll, Donncha O'Callaghan and David Wallace get to grips with Davit Zirakashvili

Ian Dowling losing the numbers game

"We're delighted with the result. There is a thin line between winning and losing, particularly in a competition like this, and to get a bonus point against a side such as that is exceptional"

Declan Kidney

No way through

O'Gara slips past Clermont's Alexandre

8 December 2007

Match 3

Llanelli Scarlets 16 – 29 Munster
Stradey Park

Digging deep when it matters most

Match report, 10 December 2007

A N AMAZING Heineken Cup night at Stradey Park. Was a game ever contested in such vile conditions and is there another forward pack who could have coped with playing into the elements as well as Munster?

They dug deep when it mattered most to pull off a 29-16 victory in the Llanelli Scarlets' famed backyard.

It moved them to the top of Pool 5 with 10 points, one ahead of London Wasps and Clermont Auvergne, and with just a single away game out of the remaining three to fulfil.

The job is far from done but confidence is running high after a superb team performance that contained magnificent individual contributions from Ronan O'Gara, Lifeimi Mafi and Shaun Payne among the backs and Anthony Foley, Denis Leamy, John Hayes and Donncha O'Callaghan up front.

None of the 10,456 hardy souls in Stradey on Saturday night will forget the rain and hail storm that lashed the ground for a seven or eight minute spell shortly after half time and sent them scurrying home in their thousands long before the finish. It also turned the pitch into a soggy mess. Munster were playing into the teeth of the elements and defending as best they could a 22-10 lead.

There were periods in both halves when Munster's grip on the game was anything but secure. A superb try for Regan King saw the Scarlets 10-6 in front after 24 minutes when they were playing into the fierce wind and rain. And after falling 22-10 behind at the interval, they had a penalty to make it 22-19 on the hour. But young replacement out-half Rhys Priestland missed from a favourable spot and Munster were quick to take advantage and went on to dominate the rest of the game.

"I think great composure was shown and all credit to the leaders like Ronan, Anthony Foley, Mick O'Driscoll and all the leaders that are in there," said Munster coach Declan Kidney.

LLANELLI SCARLETS:

M Stoddart
M Jones
R King
G Evans
N Brew
R Priestland
D Peel
I Thomas
J Hayter
D Manu
A Eustace
S MacLeod
S Easterby (capt)
G Thomas
D Jones

Replacements:

A Popham (Easterby 6-13 & 31-39 min) Jones (50 min)
V Cooper (Eustace 50 min)
J Davies (Brew 62min)
B Douglas (Stoddart 75min)
C Thomas (Priestland 76min)
D George
G Cattle

MUNSTER:

S Payne
B Carney
L Mafi
R Tipoki
I Dowling
R O'Gara (capt)
P Stringer
M Horan
J Flannery
J Hayes
D O'Callaghan
M O'Driscoll
D Leamy
D Wallace
A Foley

Replacements:

F Sheahan (Flannery 64 min)
T Buckley
D Ryan
J Coughlan (Wallace 82 min)
G Hurley
P Warwick (Payne 82 min)
K Lewis

Referee:

W Barnes (England)

SCORING	1st Half	7 mins: O'Gara pen 0-3; 15 mins: O'Gara pen 0-6; 19 mins: Priestland pen 3-6; 26 mins: King try, Priestland con 10-6; 31 mins: O'Gara pen 10-9; 35 mins: O'Gara pen 10-12; 38 mins: Wallace try, O'Gara con 10-19; 40 mins(+4): O'Gara pen 10-22 Half Time 10-22
	2nd Half	51 mins: Priestland pen 13-22; 59 mins: Priestland pen 16-22; 73 mins: Horan try, O'Gara con 16-29 Full Time 16-29

Match 3

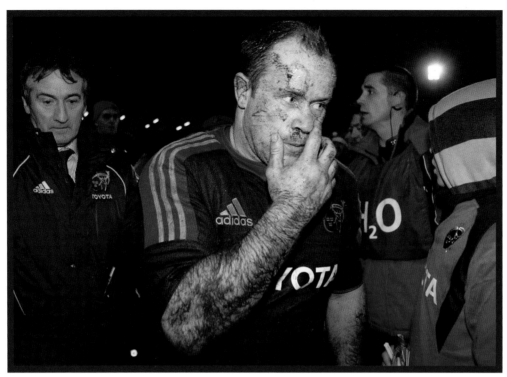

A mud-splattered Frank Sheahan

"We learned lessons last week against Leinster and stayed a bit more patient this week."

He added: "A lead of six against Llanelli is dangerous the way they play.

"I don't think having the wind meant too much to them because they are not too reliant on a kicking game. You saw how dangerous they were in the first half although they got a particularly soft try."

In fairness, the movement finished off by Regan King was a lot more than that. A misplaced kick gave Mark Jones the opportunity to set up the attack from deep in his own half and the support play and handling was really top drawer stuff.

However, O'Gara's accuracy with the boot combined with an opportunistic try for David Wallace after a piece of quick thinking by Peter

Stringer helped to redress the 10-6 imbalance and put Munster 22-10 ahead at the interval.

Wallace's score developed after Shaun Payne had displayed remarkable dexterity in getting out of a decidedly tricky situation in his own 22 before launching a raking clearance that obliged Rhys Priestland to make a hurried clearance to touch just outside his own line.

Twelve points was a handy cushion going into the second half, even against the rain and hail that lashed players and fans alike. It was then that the Munster pack, as O'Gara put it, "fronted up" with nobody happier in the going than the born again Anthony Foley.

"His performance was just typical of the man," glowed O'Gara. "These are his conditions and that's not being disrespectful to him. He's been

O'Callaghan's ball

playing this game for 15 years with Shannon since the days of the old AIL when they used to kick lumps out of each other and that's exactly what tonight was about. He's also a great sounding board and I think it was hugely important that he led the pack really well."

Another to silence his critics was Denis Leamy who seemed to be everywhere and was especially effective in a remarkable spell late in the game after Marcus Horan had grabbed a second Munster try that put the issue beyond doubt at

29-16. Leamy's ball handling as the rain bucketed down was one major reason why Munster managed 31 phases of play without losing possession.

It drained the will from the Scarlets who also had two men (Mark Jones and Deacon Manu) dispatched to the bin as against Munster's Lifeimi Mafi penalised for not rolling away after a magnificent recovery tackle on Dwayne Peel in the first half.

Lifeimi Mafi runs out of space

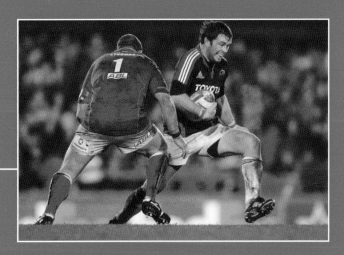

Marcus Horan and
Iestyn Thomas

Donncha O'Callaghan challenges Adam Eustace

"They've all grown up together, they've lived in the community – then that community comes together in the Heineken Cup. This side can go anywhere in the world and win and I don't know if I can say that about any other team"

Jim Williams

16 December 2007

Match 4

Munster 22 – 13 Llanelli Scarlets
Thomond Park

A giant step on the road

Match report, 17 December 2007

M UNSTER took another giant step on the road to Heineken Cup glory at Thomond Park yesterday, but, after being on the ropes a few times, will remember this scrap for a long time.

Munster coach Declan Kidney had indicated his team was not targeting a bonus point, the focus firmly on a win given the quality of the opposition.

Kidney's respect for Llanelli was well founded: "they're much better than their record in this year's competition suggests. "I'm just happy that we have taken eight points from two matches against a quality side.

"It was always about the results, not about the bonus points," he said.

But it was a deserved win, a point conceded by the Llanelli coach Phil Davies who admitted: "Munster took their chances and that was really the difference."

For the second week in succession, Munster had to lift their game in the second half when playing against the wind.

All through they dominated Llanelli out of touch, pushed them around a bit in the scrums, but once again it was the ability to hold on to possession through the phases that impressed most.

Jerry Flannery, Donncha O'Callaghan, Denis Leamy, Anthony Foley and David Wallace were in powerful form and the Scarlets could not match them enough to secure a platform for Stephen Jones.

The Welsh international did make a mark with a fine individual first-half try, but he often had to scramble clearances under pressure and rarely got the opportunity to launch counter-offences.

Munster made a lively start with man-of-the-match Rua Tipoki producing a good early steal on Jonathan Davies and they chalked down the first try six minutes into the fray.

O'Gara swung a skip pass out to the left for hooker Jerry Flannery to shrug off the tackles of Nathan Brew and Morgan Stoddart and squirm over in the corner.

Television match official Geoff Warren confirmed the grounding and while the wind forced O'Gara to drop kick the conversion after the ball fell over on his run-up, the Scarlets soon breezed up the other end for a crowd-silencing seven-pointer.

MUNSTER:
S Payne
B Carney
L Mafi
R Tipoki
I Dowling
R O'Gara (capt)
P Stringer
F Pucciariello
J Flannery
J Hayes
D O'Callaghan
M O'Driscoll
D Leamy
D Wallace
A Foley

Replacements:
F Sheahan
M Horan (Pucciariello 52 min)
D Ryan (O'Driscoll 64 min)
N Ronan
G Hurley
P Warwick
K Lewis

LLANELLI SCARLETS:
M Stoddart
M Jones
R King
J Davies
N Brew
S Jones
D Peel
I Thomas
J Hayter
B Broster
V Cooper
A Eustace
S Easterby (capt)
J Bater
A Popham

Replacements:
D Manu (Stoddart 35/40 & 4 min) (Broster 58 min)
C Thomas (M Jones 48 min)
S Macleod (Eustace 58 min)
G Thomas (Bater 58 min)
D George
N Thomas (Popham 84 min)
G Cattle

Referee:
D Pearson (England)

SCORING		
	1st Half	**5 mins:** J Flannery try 5-0; **11 mins:** S Jones try and con 5-7; **16 mins:** O'Gara pen 8-7; **24 mins:** O'Gara pen 11-7; **34 mins:** O'Gara pen 14-7; Half Time 14-7
	2nd Half	**52 mins:** Jones pen 14-10; **61 mins:** O'Gara pen 17-10; **63 mins:** Jones pen 17-13; **73 mins:** Carney try 22-13 Full Time 22-13

Jerry Flannery scores Munster's first try

The score came from a solid Scarlets scrum and although there were question marks over whether James Bater had blocked O'Gara off the ball, Jones managed to race in behind the posts on an arcing 20-metre burst.

Jones' successful conversion was cancelled out four minutes later when O'Gara landed his first penalty and two more place kicks from their stand-in captain after 24 and 34 minutes nudged Munster 14-7 clear.

Still, the Scarlets continued to look menacing, and it took a timely intervention from Peter Stringer and Brian Carney to thwart a promising attack.

Llanelli lost Ben Broster (yellow card) for 10 minutes, but managed to frustrate Munster as they gallantly defended with 14 men.

Their courage was amply demonstrated when they held out for a six minute spell on their own line at the end of the half.

Munster made a statement of intent early in the second half when they drove Llanelli back 10 metres in a scrum, but after winning a penalty, they lost concentration and possession. Then, when they conceded one, Jones made them pay to bring his side to within four points.

The kickers exchanged third- quarter penalties to leave it 17-13 to Munster, with the former champions now having to play with 14 men after substitute Marcus Horan was yellow carded for punching Deacon Manu off the ball.

It was nail-biting stuff as Munster were forced to defend valiantly in the closing stages.

However, with John Hayes coming up with a crucial steal on Vernon Cooper and Munster finally finding some space out wide, Tipoki, Mafi and Payne combined to put Carney over for the clinching score in the right corner.

Although O'Gara's conversion attempt was off target, Munster had enough in the tank to see out a vital win.

Denis Leamy gets up ahead of Vernon Cooper

Thomond Park under construction

Llanelli's Morgan Stoddart stopped by Ronan O'Gara and Mick O'Driscoll

Rua Tipoki tackled by Regan King
and Jonathan Davies

Ian Dowling hauled down by Nathan Brew

A watching brief

Marcus Horan sees yellow

Donnacha Ryan on the charge

"Munster, as ever, kept their best for adversity in a fractious Heineken blow-out. Switching, Peter Stringer released Ronan O'Gara whose marvellous, flat, delivery allowed Rua Tipoki knife through a butter defence and feed Shaun Payne who put Brian Carney over.

Popham was yellow-carded following an end-zone, apres-try, skirmish as, suddenly, the Scarlets challenge had subsided from four points behind and a man up, to nine points adrift, Popham binned and Horan about to return.

At that moment 2007 was firmly laid to rest; 2008 beckons…"

Brian Carney's try in the seventy-third minute

Anthony Foley with son Tony

13 January 2008

Match 5

ASM Clermont Auvergne 26 – 19 Munster

Parc des Sports Marcel Michelin

A precious pressure point

Match report, 14 January 2008

WHEN Munster fell 17 points behind a rampant Clermont Auvergne team with 25 minutes still to play at the splendid Parc des Sports Marcel Michelin yesterday, there was every reason to fear a defeat of embarrassing proportions.

At that stage Munster's task appeared hopeless.

Not for the first time, however, they summoned up reserves of courage and fortitude that have so long made them a major force in European rugby, forced the French on to the back foot, racked up the scores that got them to within seven points of the French and eked out the bonus point that sees them needing to beat Wasps by eight or more points at Thomond Park on Saturday to ensure they go through to the knock-out stages. They may still go through with a two point winning margin, but we're into head-to-head tries and aggregate scores for that.

That's the reward for a typically plucky performance in the last 20 minutes highlighted by a superbly taken try by Lifeimi Mafi after Munster had counter-attacked in magnificent fashion from their own 22. It's still a big ask, not least because John Hayes suffered a shoulder knock that caused him to withdraw midway through the second half and makes him doubtful for Saturday.

Furthermore, Paul O'Connell is definitely out with coach Declan Kidney indicating that it will be at least two weeks before he could again be considered.

Kidney was tight-lipped when the subject of the badly cut ear sustained by Ronan O'Gara was raised but there is little doubt that he was the victim of foul play. The culprit escaped but three of his team-mates, Loic Jacquet, Julien Malzieu and Alexandre Audebert were not so fortunate. All were binned by the English referee Rob Debney who belied his relative inexperience at this level by handling a fiercely contested clash bravely and honestly. Many of his decisions infuriated the home fans and he certainly could not have been accused of being a "homer."

However, the failure of Munster to take advantage of having three members of the opposing side off the field for a total of 30 minutes clearly disappointed a downbeat Kidney. However he took solace from the fact that his side took something from a game that he accepts was dominated by Clermont for the opening 32 minutes and for other stages later in the proceedings.

ASM CLERMONT AUVERGNE:

A Floch
A Rougerie (capt)
M Joubert
S Bai
J Malzieu
B James
P Mignoni
L Emmanuelli
M Ledesma
M Scelzo
A Jacquet
T Privat
J Bonnaire
A Audebert
E Vermeulen

Replacements:

S Broomhall (Bonnaire 43-46 min) (Vermeulen 65 min)
D Zirakashvili (Scelzo 47 min)
C Samson (Privat 62 min)
B Baby (Bai 67 min)
M Lozupone
J Senio
V Delasau

MUNSTER:

S Payne
B Carney
R Tipoki
L Mafi
D Howlett
R O'Gara
P Stringer (capt)
M Horan
J Flannery
J Hayes
D O'Callaghan
M O'Driscoll
D Leamy
D Wallace
A Foley

Replacements:

F Sheahan
T Buckley (Hayes 58 min)
D Ryan
A Quinlan (Foley 65 min)
T O'Leary
P Warwick
K Lewis

Referee:

R Debney (England)

SCORING   1st Half   **11 mins:** O'Gara pen 0-3; **18 mins:** Mignoni try, James con 7-3; **25 mins:** James pen 10-3; **32 mins:** James pen 13-3; **34 mins:** Ledesma try, James con 20-3; **40(+6) mins:** O'Gara pen 20-6
Half Time 20-6
2nd Half   **57 mins:** James pen 23-6; **60 mins:** Mafi try, O'Gara con 23-13; **71 mins:** O'Gara pen 23-16; **77 mins:** O'Gara pen 23-19; **80 mins:** James pen 26-19
Full Time 26-19

Reverse offload from Jerry Flannery
in the tackle

Horan snaffled by Marius Joubert and Thibaut Privat

But he warned: "We won't have a chance against the reigning champions (Wasps) if we don't play a lot better than that.

"I would never question the spirit and honesty of the players but that doesn't cover up why we were so far off the mark today. We will look at what went wrong."

There were one or two glimpses of Doug Howlett's class and Lifeimi Mafi took his crucial try in style. The introduction of replacements Tony Buckley and Alan Quinlan for the final quarter or so also helped the cause.

Munster certainly couldn't complain about a 20-6 half time lead for the French. Their intensity was absolutely ferocious and rocked the visitors back on their heels. Even though O'Gara put Munster ahead with a 10th minute penalty and also finished the first half with a second goal

kick, in between it was all Clermont; and at times it took desperate defence to keep the big men up front and fliers like Aurelien Rougerie, Julien Malzieu and Seremaia Bai, at bay.

Something had to give, of course, and the inevitable came to pass on 19 minutes when will-of-the-wisp scrum-half Pierre Mignoni wriggled his way over close to the Munster posts after strong pressure and Brock James tapped over the conversion. Even at this early stage, it was clear that the Munster scrum was in dire straits, paving the way for James to knock over a penalty. With a seven point advantage safely banked away, Clermont were happy to spread it wide and test the Munster defensive will.

They gave it their all, not least on the half hour when somehow preventing Elvis Vermeulen from getting the touch down after he was blasted over the Munster line by a whole regiment of colleagues. Nevertheless, the French took three points from the attack courtesy of another James penalty and a distinctly embarrassing day looked to be evolving when Mario Ledesma crashed over in the 34th minute, James converting.

Mafi did cross the Clermont line in the 39th minute but referee Rob Debney quite rightly ruled no score and instead awarded a close range penalty for a previous infringement. Munster opted for a scrum and in the ensuing melee the home second-row Loic Jacquet was yellow carded.

The pressure was maintained but David Wallace and Marcus Horan were held up just short and Munster had only O'Gara's second penalty to show for all their effort.

Jacquet was joined in the bin immediately after the restart by Malzieu when he deliberately knocked on a potential scoring pass from Rua Tipoki to Brian Carney. This was another decent Munster spell but their inability to capitalise on having Clermont reduced to 13 players hurt them badly. If anything, that they were out-muscled in a couple of mauls did wonders for Clermont morale.

After one such assault, Munster were penalised and James again found the target.

At 23-6 down and 25 minutes still to play, it was looking ominous indeed for Munster. But then their traditional heart and courage came to the fore and produced a result that keeps alive their hopes of a tenth successive quarter-final place.

Referee Rob Debney in safe hands

O'Callaghan forces the knock on

Rougerie closes in on
Doug Howlett

Wallace lays it off

Bruised but unbowed

"So Munster keep the Irish flag flying. They've conducted themselves with intelligence, skill and bravery, not least away to Clermont, and seemingly have an in-built compass to navigate just such a choppy pool of sharks"

Gerry Thornley *The Irish Times*

19 January 2008

Match 6

Munster 19 – 3 London Wasps
Thomond Park

The Perfect 10 kicks Wasps off their throne

Match report, 21 January 2008

RONAN O'GARA made Thomond Park his stage once again on Saturday with a display that shattered the hopes of Heineken Cup champions London Wasps and steered his Munster team into the knock-out stages of this marvellous tournament for an incredible 10th successive year.

Donncha O'Callaghan was voted man-of-the-match and he had a magnificent game, as did all eight forwards on a night of high pressure and relentless rain which drained the last drop of energy from each participant.

Standing on a different pedestal, however, was O'Gara. He showed his burning resolution and a very smart turn of speed in the 14th minute to outpace Wasps winger David Doherty and prevent a certain try. He went on to kick five goals from five attempts on a quagmire of a pitch where keeping one's feet alone was a major challenge. Then there was the manner in which he mixed his tactical kicking. Time and again he confused and unsettled the Wasps defence before late in the game he scythed his way through in classical out-half fashion before delivering a perfect scoring pass to Denis Leamy.

And, let's not forget his captaincy of the victorious team. He has grown into the job so well that he is now entitled to his place in the pantheon of great Munster leaders like Mick Galwey, Jim Williams, Anthony Foley and Paul O'Connell.

High praise, indeed, but well merited. Just about everyone at Thomond Park on Saturday were absorbed by the majesty of O'Gara's display.

Even Wasps captain Lawrence Dallaglio agreed that "Ronan O'Gara knows how to play a lead, especially on his own pitch".

Dallaglio's director of rugby Ian McGeechan and coach Shaun Edwards saw things in a similar light.

McGeechan: "Ronan O'Gara was the difference. He put the forwards in the right place and ensured they played the game in the right part of the field."

Edwards went even further: "If I hadn't been coaching Wasps, I would almost have stood up and applauded O'Gara because I thought he was superb in the second half. The variety of his kicking, his control of the game; it was a marvellous performance by a number 10 in great form."

MUNSTER:
S Payne
B Carney
R Tipoki
L Mafi
D Howlett
R O'Gara (capt)
P Stringer
M Horan
J Flannery
J Hayes
D O'Callaghan
M O'Driscoll
D Leamy
D Wallace
A Foley

Replacements:
F Sheahan (Flannery 82 min)
T Buckley
D Ryan
A Quinlan (Foley 77 min)
T O'Leary
P Warwick
K Lewis

LONDON WASPS:
J Lewsey
D Doherty
F Waters
R Hoadley
D Waldouck
D Cipriani
E Reddan
T Payne
R Ibañez
P Vickery
S Shaw
G Skivington
J Haskell
T Rees
L Dallaglio (capt)

Replacements:
T Palmer (Shaw 48 min)
R Webber (Rees 61 min)
J Ward (Ibañez 76 min)
T French (Payne 82 min)
J Hart
M McMillan
D Walder

Referee:
N Owens (Wales)

SCORING	1st Half	5 mins: Cipriani 0-3; 12 mins: O'Gara pen 3-3;
		37 mins: O'Gara pen 6-3; 40 (+7) mins: O'Gara pen 9-3
		Half Time 9-3
	2nd Half	54 mins: O'Gara pen 12-3; 74 mins: Leamy try, O'Gara con 19-3
		Full Time 19-3

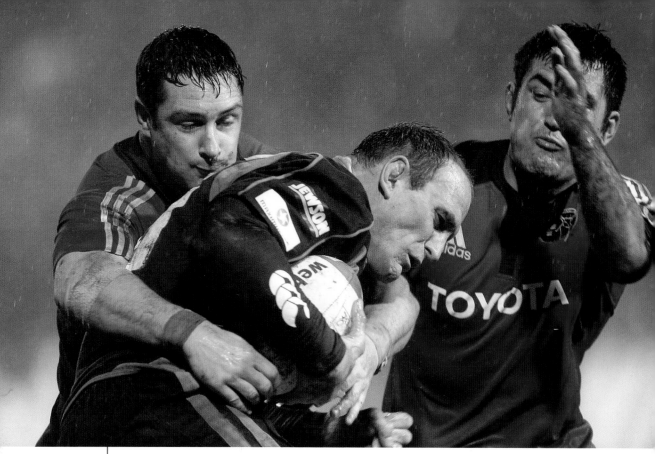

Even that was nothing compared with how his long term-mentor and tough taskmaster Declan Kidney reacted to this latest tour de force.

"I thought Ronan was absolutely magnificent. I couldn't speak highly enough of the man. His match management and the way he played through was exceptional. A huge amount of credit is due to him."

O'Gara stressed how "huge an achievement it was for the squad" and went back to the previous week to laud the players for leaving Clermont with the bonus point that kept them in the competition. On a personal note, he underlined how he "has really enjoyed the captaincy although during the week I was thinking that if we didn't qualify, I'd be the first captain in 10 years not to lead Munster into the quarter-finals and that was pressure on my shoulders."

He outlined how, at the captain's meeting, he had asked the forwards for a big performance and they had delivered.

And he went on: "The sum of the parts in Munster is always greater than the individual but there are some cracking athletes and rugby players so once you have that will to win, the character and the desire for each other makes it a good formula."

O'Gara's point about his captaincy is well made. He had a few tough calls to make, notably one on the stroke of the interval when the referee told him he had time for a scrum or a kick at goal but not for a line-out. He took the responsibility on himself from way out on the right and nervelessly drilled a difficult kick between the sticks to open a six points lead (9-3).

O'Gara's brilliant all-round play and goal kicking pushed Munster 12-3 ahead after 53 minutes and while it was looking good, the fear was always present that Wasps would grab a try and sneak past the home side in the qualification stakes.

My ball, thank you!

So when they pitched camp deep in the Wasps 22 with 10 minutes to play, Munster were determined to stay there.

They reeled off the phases much as they had done in similar conditions at Llanelli.

This time, there were 22 in all as they all handled the bar of soap with absolute perfection. Finally, the Wasps defence cracked.

"The forwards were wearing them down and wearing them down and when I saw Ibanez and Redser as the second last defender, I just kept running and somebody shot out of the line and then I off-loaded to Leams and he did the rest," O'Gara said.

"To get the try then was a massive relief because of the quality of Wasps. If they got it to 12-8, 12-10, we'd win the game but they'd go through."

At 19-3, though, that fear was extinguished and in spite of late Wasps pressure, the soaked supporters knew it was a done deal well before the final whistle and joyously belted out "The Fields" and "Stand Up and Fight" with rare gusto.

Finally, in lavishing praise on O'Gara, I would hate to give the impression that was a one-man band. The out-half would be first to point out that he couldn't have performed to this level without the support of every one of his teammates.

Wasps are a fine side and had reason to feel hard done by at the sin binning of Simon Shaw for not retiring 10 metres at a Munster penalty close to their posts. Ian McGeechan felt Nigel Owens might have been trying to square the deal as he had already binned Denis Leamy. Later, Mr Owens put none other than the ever chatting Lawrence Dallaglio in his place leaving the game's most talkative one to cool his heels for 10 minutes.

But Munster maintained their discipline much better than Wasps, a point forcibly made by Kidney, who rightly stressed that the glory rested with the entire squad. O'Gara may have stood out but that doesn't mean you argue with Donncha O'Callaghan's man-of-the-match award.

He has developed into one of the game's great tacklers and work horses and is only getting better.

Much the same can be said of Shaun Payne who brought off one catch that would have impressed if not actually astonished the most ardent of Kerry football fans and there were indications, too, of what Doug Howlett can mean to this team.

"He's not regarded as one of the great All Blacks for nothing," said O'Gara.

This was Munster's best performance of the campaign and it's only a pity, as the captain pointed out, that they won't play together again for 10 weeks. "We've been in a hard group, the momentum is there, and it would be great to try and continue this competition but that's not the way it is," he regretted.

Doug Howlett powers through

Seeing it through Munster tinted glasses

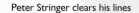

Peter Stringer clears his lines

"They just keep rolling along. For the 10th year in a row Munster made their way to the quarter final of the Heineken Cup here and they did it the way they've always done. Bit by little bit, inch by little inch"

Malachy Clerkin *The Sunday Tribune*

Doug Howlett is brought down by Josh Lewsey

Man of the Match, Donncha O'Callaghan contesting the lineout

Are you serious?

Tipoki brings down Lewsey

A determined Brian Carney

Safe hands from Mick O'Driscoll

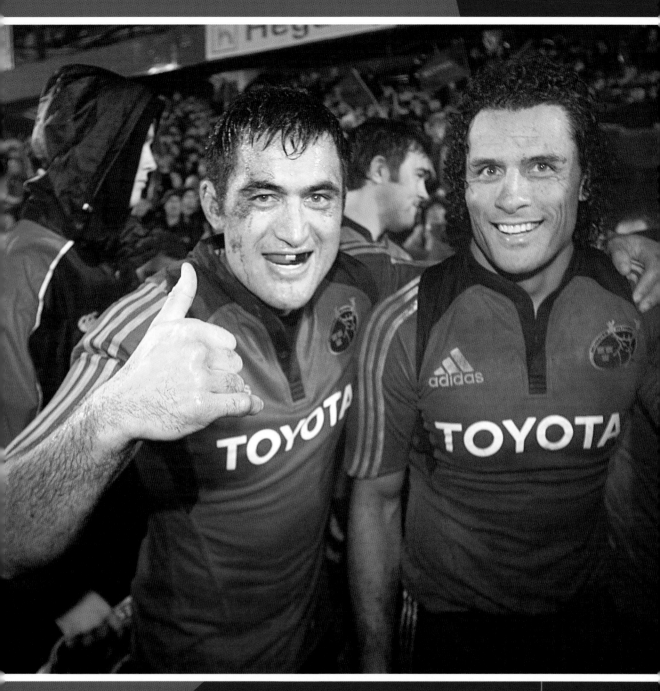

Thumbs up

Red Army in full flow

Denis Leamy scores the decisive try

THE QUARTER FINAL

Match 7

5 April 2008

Gloucester 3 – 16 Munster
Kingsholm

A famous victory on the road

Match report, 7 April 2008

GLOUCESTER
O Morgan
C Paterson
J Simpson-Daniel
A Allen
L Vainikolo
R Lamb
R Lawson
N Wood
A Titterrell
C Nieto
M Bortolami (capt)
A Brown
P Buxton
A Hazell
L Narraway

Replacements:
G Delve (Buxton 34-40 & 51min)
M Tindall (Allen 40 min)
J Paul (Titterrell 56-63 min)
W Walker (Paterson 58 min)
W James (Bortolami 56 min)
A Dickinson (Wood 67 min)
G Cooper (Lawson 67 min)

MUNSTER:
D Hurley
D Howlett
R Tipoki
L Mafi
I Dowling
R O'Gara
T O'Leary
T Buckley
J Flannery
J Hayes
D O'Callaghan
P O'Connell (capt)
A Quinlan
D Wallace
D Leamy

Replacements:
F Sheahan
F Pucciariello (Buckley 33 min)
M O'Driscoll (Wallace 82 min)
A Foley (Leamy 77 min)
P Stringer
P Warwick
K Lewis

Referee:
N Owens (Wales)

DECLAN KIDNEY has proved many, many times that he has the Midas Touch but Saturday's events at Kingsholm surpassed most things that had gone before. He has now led his Munster team to their seventh Heineken Cup semi-final and a clash with Alan Gaffney's Saracens, yesterday's surprise though deserving winners over the Ospreys, a game that will be played at Coventry City's Ricoh Arena on Sunday, April 27.

"An occasion I will really cherish, it will be some experience," was Gaffney's, the Munster coach for three seasons, take on the clash to come.

Kidney, for his part, recognised last night: "Saracens will get momentum from this result and, of course, Alan is a brilliant coach and would know us inside out."

Close observers of the Heineken Cup scene were gobsmacked when Kidney dropped Peter Stringer, especially, and Shaun Payne, for the quarter-final clash with English Premiership leaders Gloucester at Kingsholm and replaced them with two apparent greenhorns in Tomás O'Leary and Denis Hurley.

Kidney believed he could strengthen the side still further by giving O'Leary only his second start in the competition at number nine and by calling up Hurley, who hadn't even sat on a European bench up to that point.

However it worked like a dream. O'Leary kicked, ran and tackled like a man possessed and fulfilled his primary role with distinction.

Hurley brought, youth, courage and footballing nous to the table in spades. He pulled off at least one try-saving tackle on dangerman James Simpson-Daniel, fielded the high ball impeccably and capped it all with a glorious grubber kick to set up the second try for Doug Howlett.

Kidney was perfectly entitled to take a bow but that is not his form.

Words like "gamble" and expressions like "rolling the dice" were bandied about once the team was announced but he wasn't seeking any justification for his selection. "It's nothing to do with me," he claimed. "I'm just fronting up here working with a

SCORING   1st Half   **14 mins:** O'Gara pen 0-3; **40 mins:** Dowling try 0-8;
                             Half Time 0-8
         2nd Half   **50 mins:** O'Gara pen 0-11; **64 mins:** Howlett try 0-16;
                             70 mins: Lamb pen 3-16
                             Full Time 3-16

Match 7

superb bunch of people. There are 41 players and we sat down last Tuesday and said that we want to be here next Tuesday and still in the competition. We have a backroom team that is always cajoling me and saying, do this with them, do that with them, back off them here, back off them there, and I'm just representative of that. That's what today was all about, just a great squad effort by everybody on the pitch, lads who didn't make the pitch, and everybody in the backroom team."

All true, of course, but even in a quintessential team game like rugby, the more successful teams will always have stand-out players on a given day. There is no doubt that Hurley and O'Leary slotted comfortably into that category at Kingsholm but there were others as well with Kidney happy to refer to Doug Howlett's part in developing the new full-back's game.

"Doug has been very good to Denis over the last number of weeks," he noted. "They've been sitting down and going through stuff and learning things off one another.

Not alone did Doug have his own performance but the way he has helped Denis is a huge credit to him."

Sky gave Rua Tipoki the man of the match award and he certainly had a tremendous game highlighted by one amazing turnover and some great tackling. But no game is won without a mighty effort by the forwards.

Apart from the scrum, which was in some disarray early on largely due to Marcus Horan's late withdrawal, they eventually gained the upper hand after an ominously slow start.

Denis Hurley on his Heineken debut

Rua Tipoki

Howlett delivers

Paul O'Connell confronts
Luke Narraway

Lifeimi Mafi with support

As Kidney noted: "We didn't have the ball for the first 12 minutes."

But once the big guns got going, the trend changed completely. And outstanding in all of this were Alan Quinlan, who seemed to be just about everywhere as he fearlessly carried the battle to Gloucester, and Paul O'Connell, a man clearly benefiting from an extended run after such a frustratingly long period out through injury.

But there was still a lot of defending to be done and for my money that's where this Munster team shone brightest. Some of the tackles were bone-crushing with Lifeimi Mafi bringing the house down with a fearsome hit on Gloucester hooker Andy Titterall. But it was just one of many that must have warmed the heart of defence coach Tony McGahan.

O'Connell insisted this was "an honest effort"

from one to 15. "This is a great jersey to play in," he smiled.

The game's two tries were touched down by wingers Ian Dowling and Doug Howlett. Both were superbly created and executed with the Gloucester defence opened up on both occasions with vital contributions from Tipoki, Mafi and with the try scorers themselves involved in the build-up.

Ronan O'Gara, who again looked the finished article in a fine display in both defence and attack, shaved the posts with both conversions and also knocked over a couple of penalties.

When Ryan Lamb was instructed to kick for goal with his side 16-0 behind and 11 minute still showing on the clock, Gloucester were already accepting defeat as their lot.

Tipoki gets it away

Dowling beats the tackle

"All you could do yesterday was study the perplexed face of Ryan afterwards and listen to the words he used. For Munster he chose "accomplished" and "admiration" and praised their "very physical, outstanding defence." His own side, in contrast, were heading in the right direction but still had much to learn. And it all led back to the words he had uttered earlier in the week. Against such a mighty force, as Ryan knew deep down, his side never stood a chance"

John O'Brien *Sunday Independent*

O'Leary takes the quick tap

It takes two

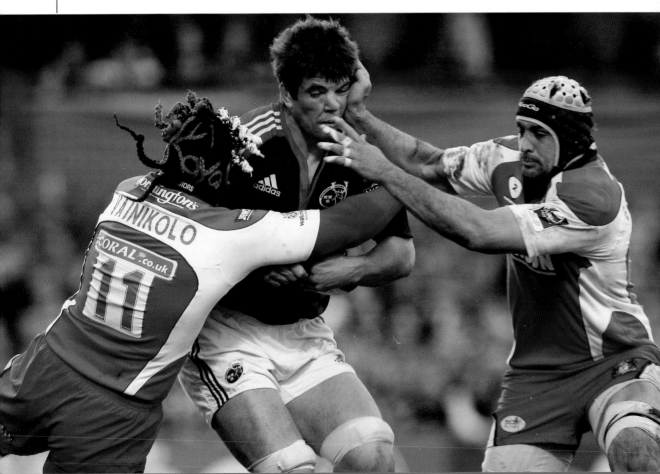

Dowling scores the
opening try

Federico Pucciariello tackles
Rory Lawson

Line-out ball

Alan Quinlan

O'Leary brought down to earth

Ruck ball

Putting out the volcano

Semi-final beckons

Match 7

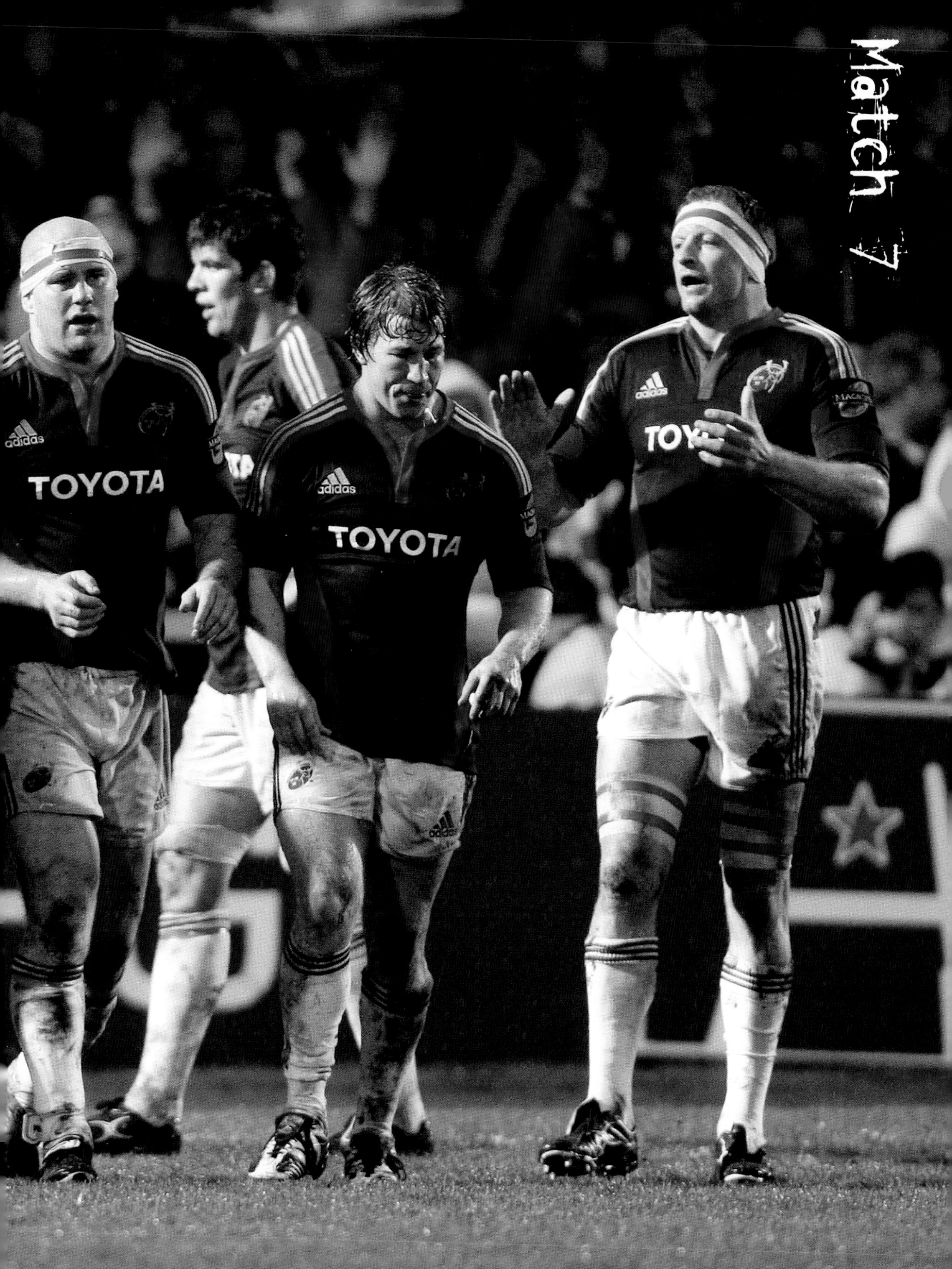

Howlett grounds a second

No he didn't!

"The odyssey continues, the great adventure goes on. What Jack Charlton's inspirational Irish soccer team were to the earliest years of the emerging Celtic Tiger Ireland of the late eighties and early nineties, Declan Kidney's magnificent Munster rugby team are fast becoming to the final years of the noughties"

Jim Glennon *Sunday Independent*

Party time in Kingsholm

27 April 2008

Saracens 16 – 18 Munster

The Ricoh Arena

Too close for comfort

Match report, 28 April 2008

THIS was far too close for comfort for Munster and their fans. Somehow, they held out for victory in yesterday's Heineken Cup semi-final, in spite of being on the ropes for much of the game and especially five nail-biting minutes at the finish that none of the 30,325 spectators inside this splendid stadium will quickly forget.

It wasn't that 7/4 on favourites Munster played poorly, more a case of Saracens, under Alan Gaffney, once again raising their game for the European scene. Few would have begrudged them had a late, fierce assault earned them a winning score. Making it all the more emotional from a Saracens viewpoint was that the heroic World Cup winner Richard Hill was playing his last match for the club he has represented all his life and he was the one to concede a penalty at the death ending their last vestige of hope.

Munster have four weeks in which to learn the lessons of this pulsating semi-final. They will wonder whether they themselves played poorly or if it was a case of Sarries working their socks off for Hill and Gaffney, who is also leaving the club at the end of the season. Individually, the two wingers, Francisco Leonelli and Kameli Ratuvou, gave Munster countless headaches, while scrum-half and captain Neil De Kock was a battlefield general. The pack fronted up and their bitter disappointment at the end of a bruising struggle was utterly understandable. Defeat certainly would have been a bitter pill to swallow for people like Hill and Hugh Vyvyan.

"I couldn't have asked for any more from my players", said Gaffney. "We had a lot of play in their 22, but didn't put our foot on their throat."

De Koch put it quite similarly: "We shot ourselves in the foot by giving turnovers and giving away penalties."

"We got out of jail today and I wouldn't deny that," said Kidney.

"Things didn't flow for us, but we stuck in there. A few bits of class by Ronan and Quinny made a difference and once again our defence was outstanding. With Richard Hill and Alan Gaffney nearing the end of their careers at Saracens, we knew they would want to pull out a big game and that's just what they did."

SARACENS:
R Haughton
F Leonelli
K Sorrell
A Powell
K Ratuvou
G Jackson
N de Kock (capt)
N Lloyd
M Cairns
C Visagie
H Vyvyan
K Chesney
P Gustard
R Hill
B Skirving.

Replacements:
F Ongaro
C Johnston (Visagie 47 min)
T Ryder (Skirving 32 min)
D Barrell
M Rauluni (de Kock 77 min)
G Ross
D Scarborough

MUNSTER:
D Hurley
D Howlett
R Tipoki
L Mafi
I Dowling
R O'Gara
T O'Leary
M Horan
J Flannery
J Hayes
D O'Callaghan
P O'Connell (capt)
A Quinlan
D Wallace
D Leamy

Replacements:
F Sheahan
F Pucciariello
M O'Driscoll
D Ryan (O'Callaghan 74 min)
P Stringer
P Warwick
B Murphy

Referee:
N Owens (Wales)

SCORING   1st Half   **5 mins:** Ratuvou try, Jackson con 7-0; **8 mins:** O'Gara pen 7-3;
25 mins: O'Gara try 7-8; **40 mins:** Quinlan try, O'Gara con 7-15
Half Time 7-15

2nd Half   **43 mins:** Jackson pen 10-15; **57 mins:** Jackson pen 13-15;
62 mins: O'Gara pen 13-18; **71 mins:** Jackson pen 16-18

Full Time 16-18

Ricoh reception

Paul O'Connell with mascot Daniel Moloney

Hair raising support

Haughton halts Mafi

Howlett holds on

Coming through

Paul O'Connell spoke of the fierce pace of play in the opening minutes and certainly his side was hard pushed to cope.

Accordingly, it was ironic that Munster should have been swarming all over the Sarries 22 when conceding the first try of the game. Richard Haughton and Ratuvou combined down the left before centre Adam Powell took off on a diagonal run towards the posts. Doug Howlett caught him in the nick of time but, when the ball was quickly recycled, Ratuvou was unopposed as he touched down at the posts for a try that Glen Jackson converted.

O'Gara's classic out-half try on 30 minutes settled supporter's nerves somewhat but there followed some scary moments when Munster had to defend for their lives and nobody more honestly and forcibly than Tomás O'Leary and Lifeimi Mafi. As luck and perfect timing would have it, they broke out on the stroke of half time

and Doug Howlett was given the opportunity stretch his legs. He was nailed on the 22, but David Wallace got there first and opened the way for Alan Quinlan to burst out of the ruck of players and gallop over unopposed between the posts. O'Gara converted and Munster held an eight-point interval lead (15-7).

The players were greeted by heavy rain as they came out for the second half and within three minutes of the restart Jackson kicked the easy goal to leave five points separating the sides.

Referee Nigel Owens was seeing little right in Munster's approach at this point of the game. When Rua Tipoki infringed at a ruck, he was sent to the bin and Haughton converted the resultant penalty. Now, if anything, the advantage lay with Saracens. Well, for a couple of seconds anyway. Munster mauled their way down the left, Sarries prop Nick Lloyd got involved with Denis Leamy and started flailing with his fists. Off he went and within moments the referee was banishing Cencus Johnston, the prop who had just arrived in place of Visagie, for a flagrant foul in a ruck.

This time O'Gara made the kick and Munster were in the driving seat, five points up and 13 against 14. Jackson narrowed it to two again with ten minutes on the clock. It was edge-of-the-seat time, but it was then more than ever that the team's vast experience edged Munster home.

A break for Johnston

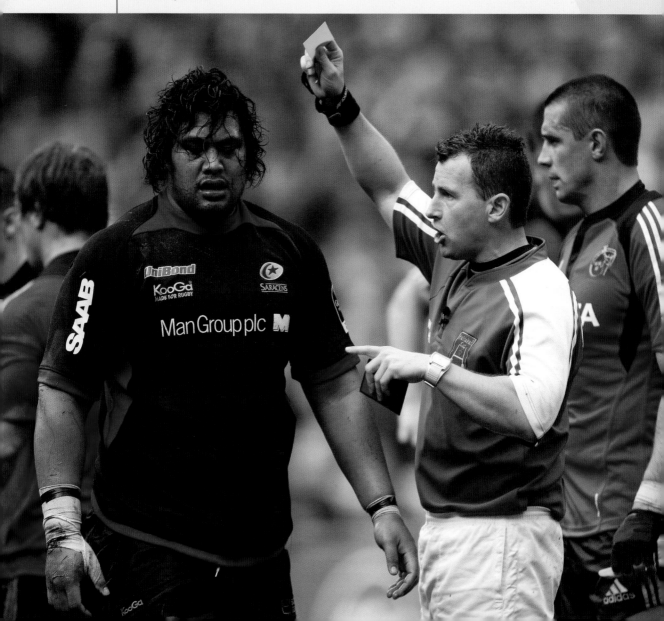

O'Gara nails another

O'Gara breaks the line

Quinlan scores the second

"Declan Kidney, Jerry Holland and Garret Fitzgerald have put in place the most talented and most balanced squad with the greatest strength in depth in Munster rugby history. For years we bemoaned the lack of creative guile and limited cutting edge outside of Ronan O'Gara. But now, at last, we are witnessing the real and near complete deal"

Tony Ward *Irish Independent*

Tomás O'Leary

John Hayes catching
his breath

Your ball Quinny

Standing shoulder to shoulder

Picking his spot

Wallace going for the gap

Mafi wrong foots Adam Powell

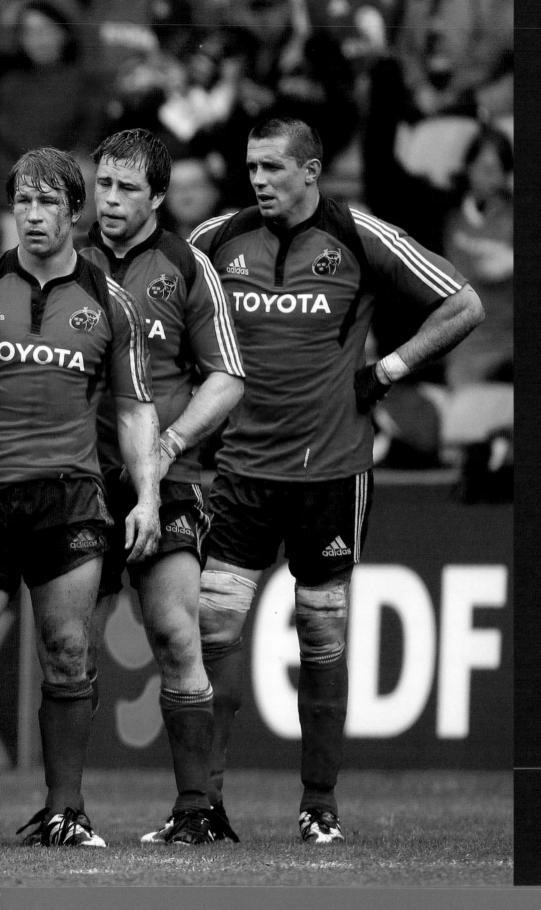

Sorting things out

Well done Tomás!

Munster's Paul O'Connell and David Wa[...]
after the final whistle

Alan Gaffney at the end of the game

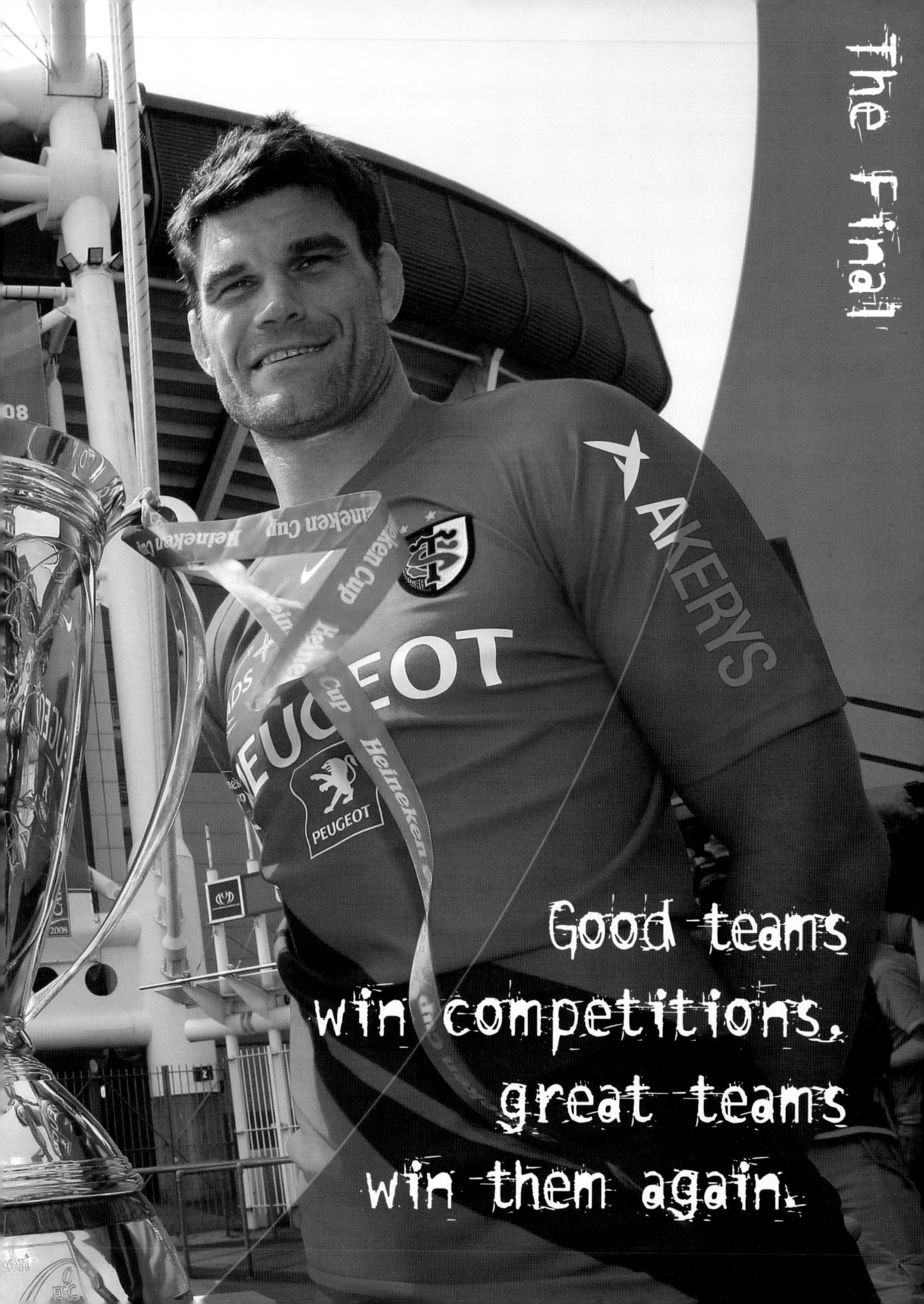

Good teams
win competitions,
great teams
win them again.

Rua Tipoki, firmly focused

Media day at UL

Williams and
McGahan keep
a watchful eye

A relaxed captain and coach

Limbering up

Young admirers

BRISTOL RUGBY   CARDIFF BLUES   EDINBURGH

Practice makes perfect

Final Training

We love you Dougie!

Outside Cardiff Castle

Countdown to the final

Spelling it out

Warming up

"These fans have done everything to make this competition, they go
everywhere. There is an affinity between players and supporters
and that's one of the things that makes a real difference"

Ronan O'Gara

Home support

THE FINAL

Match 9

24 May 2008

Munster 16 – 13 Toulouse
The Millennium Stadium

How do you top this?

Match report, 26 May 2008

TEARS of joy and sadness had many the same source shortly before 7pm on Saturday as Paul O'Connell and Ronan O'Gara raised the Heineken Cup, 60,000 Irish people cheered themselves hoarse and four great rugby men pondered just what they were leaving behind.

The fact that O'Connell insisted on O'Gara, who had captained the side through the pool stages of the competition, raising the trophy with him spoke volumes for the kind of people we're talking about here. O'Gara described the gesture as "the height of unselfishness" and another deep bond had been forged between this remarkable group of sportsmen. Further pathos was added to the occasion by the knowledge that Declan Kidney, the head coach, and Jim Williams, the forwards coach, would no longer be part of the Munster set-up as they move on to duty at the highest international levels and that two other great servants of the cause, Anthony Foley and Shaun Payne, were retiring.

Williams, a key influence for Munster for the best part of a decade, was particularly overcome and who could blame him? Munster's loss is Australia's gain. He leaves for home on Wednesday and starts his new job as assistant Aussie coach next Monday.

What now for Munster? How do you top this? The aim, no doubt, will be to conquer Europe for the second successive year but Kidney believes that should be a matter for another day. For the present, he says all associated with Munster should enjoy this latest triumph: "One of the things I personally learned the last time was that we were too busy in the aftermath of it but we're really going to enjoy this one for a month or two. How often does this come around? To have it come around once is a dream, to have it come around twice is incredible."

MUNSTER:
D Hurley
D Howlett
L Mafi
R Tipoki
I Dowling
R O'Gara
T O'Leary
M Horan
J Flannery
J Hayes
D O'Callaghan
P O'Connell (capt)
A Quinlan
D Wallace
D Leamy

Replacements:
F Sheahan
T Buckley (Horan 64-74 min)
M O'Driscoll (O'Connell 58-61 min)
D Ryan
P Stringer
P Warwick
K Earls

TOULOUSE:
C Heymans
M Medard
M Kunavore
Y Jauzion
Y Donguy
J Elissalde
B Kelleher
D Human
W Servat
S Perugini
F Pelous (capt)
P Albacete
J Bouilhou
T Dusautoir
S Sowerby

Replacements:
Y Nyanga (Dusautoir 39 min)
J-B Poux (Perugini 56 min)
R Millo-Chlusky (Albacete 62 min)
GB Lamboley (Bouilho 62 min)
M Ahotaeiloa (Donguy 72 min)
A Vernet Basualdo
F Fritz

Referee:
N Owens (Wales)

SCORING

1st Half	7 mins: Elissalde dp gl 3-0; **33 mins:** Leamy try, O'Gara con 7-3;	
	36 mins: O'Gara pen 10-3; **40 mins:** Elissalde pen 10-6;	
	Half Time 10-6	
2nd Half	**52 mins:** O'Gara pen 13-6; **54 mins:** Donguy try, Elissalde con 13-13;	
	65 mins: O'Gara pen 16-13	
	Full Time 16-13	

O'Leary and Leamy take down Kelleher

Curbing the inevitable emotion associated with the occasion was just one of the herculean tasks facing this Munster side. The survivors of the team that lost to Northampton in the 2000 decider recognise now they got too worked up prior to the game. It cost them dearly. They have long since become too experienced to fall into that trap. So they went out against the "aristocrats of Europe" with ice in their veins and never allowed their concentration to drop for a second.

Those who feel this wasn't quite the game of rugby they had anticipated or that the occasion lacked some of the exhilaration associated with the victory in this same stadium two years previously would do well to bear a few salient points in mind.

Chief among them was their pledge after the 2006 campaign that they wouldn't settle for just one European title. The mantra became: "Good teams win competitions, great teams win them again." Which brings us nicely to Toulouse. They had been crowned champions of Europe three times previously. So they were already a great team and one that Munster somehow had to conquer if they were to assume that mantle.

That's why Declan Kidney was almost giddy on Saturday night, elated by what was a truly astonishing achievement. It was like he had climbed Everest for a second time and no matter how hard he tried to conceal it, the sense of pride and achievement was bursting clean out of his chest.

His Toulouse counterpart Guy Noves paid him the ultimate compliment: "Munster deserved to win because they knew what they had to do to beat us."

Jauzion and Hurley contest a high b

Rua Tipoki

Pelous is sin binned

Essentially, it was a team performance, a point well made by the turnover scrum on the Toulouse line on the half hour that Noves singled out as "the turning point in the game". If only for that single incident, the oft-criticised Marcus Horan, Jerry Flannery, John Hayes front-row axis will be seen as being among the true heroes of the day.

It wasn't the only crucial moment in a fiercely contested game and the French captain Fabien Pelous will surely have nightmares for getting himself binned for no good reason at a crucial stage of the game.

"I did lose the head a bit but he (Alan Quinlan) did stamp on my foot but it's a shame that I should have reacted as I did at my age", he acknowledged. Ironically, Toulouse scored their try while Pelous was off the field but his 10-minute absence surely diminished their energy reserves later in the game. Noves clearly regarded it as a serious crime and made no effort to excuse Pelous's indiscretion.

Quinlan had yet another blinder and was voted Sky TV man of the match, which only goes to show how well he played, given that Paul O'Connell was back once again to his awesome best. The captain's work-rate was astonishing and he never once shirked trying to make the hard yards. The game could not have been won without a towering forward performance and that's just what the entire Munster pack produced.

Many would have gone for Peter Stringer at scrum-half ahead of Tomás O'Leary but once again Kidney was right on the money. O'Leary demonstrated that he is a chip off the old block

Catch me if you can

Marcus shows he can step

and that he could handle these major sporting occasions in the same cool, efficient manner that his father did on All-Ireland final day at Croke Park. His tactical kicking was well-nigh perfect, he cleared the ball well from the base of maul and ruck and, time and again, put his body on the line.

It is little wonder that O'Gara loves playing alongside the foreign legion of Mafi, Tipoki and Howlett. They tried every ploy from their formidable repertoire of tricks and were at least the equal of the illustrious group of players lined up against them.

The trio, the only members of the side not born in the province, were just as excited and delighted as the home contingent and that's another good reason why Munster are European champions for the second time in three years.

All told, a great bunch of players have had their just reward and, in the process, swelled the pride of a province. Perhaps even a country.

It takes two to stop Flannery

Leamy shrugs off Pelous

Stretching more than the defence

"I'd like to thank those guys who have been part of this over the past 10 years and all those who have been part of it in over 100 years of Munster rugby. We're just the lucky ones. All the work is done at the clubs and the schools and it's true that the cream comes to the top"

Declan Kidney

Quinlan comes to cover

Try time for Donguy

To the brave and the faithful nothing is impossible

Caption

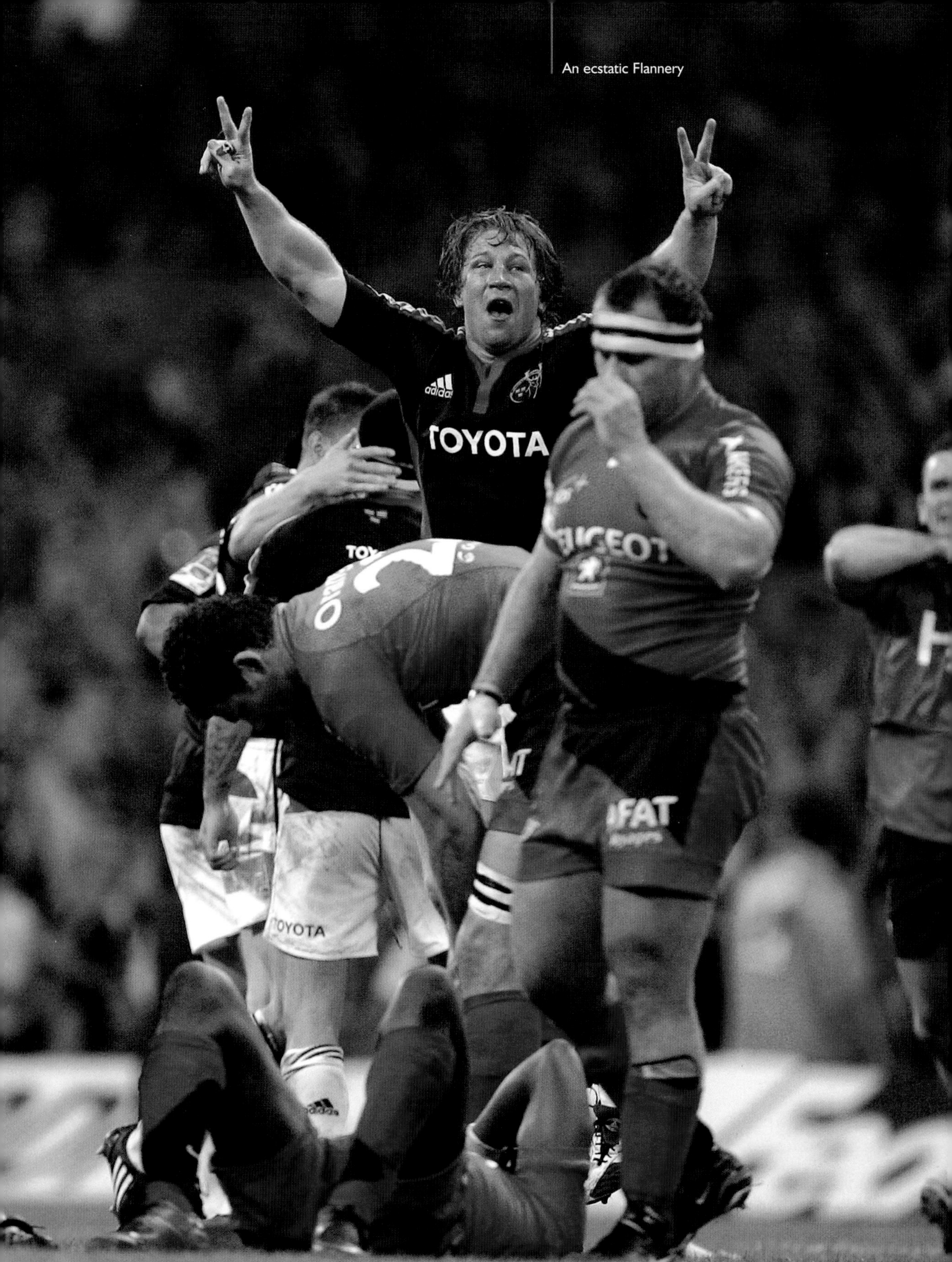

An ecstatic Flannery

TOYOTA

7

We've done it!

All embracing moment

Congratulations

Declan Kidney and Ian Dowling

"They needed to be winners again, and by beating Toulouse they knocked over the most successful team in the history of this great competition. Kidney can leave now for Ireland with a very remarkable coaching record further embellished"

Brendan Fanning *Sunday Independent*

"To become the best Munster had to beat the best, and that they did, compelling and more conclusively than the scoreline suggests. Whether one for the purists or not, only Wasps - a brilliant, all-powerful Wasps at the peak of their powers - had overcome the French aristocrats in four previous European Cup finals and that was by dint of a freakish, last-minute mugging. This, despite the scoreboard, was a more decisive beating than that and even more conclusive victory than Munster's one over Biarritz two years ago"

Gerry Thornley *The Irish Times*

Victory photocall

Match 9

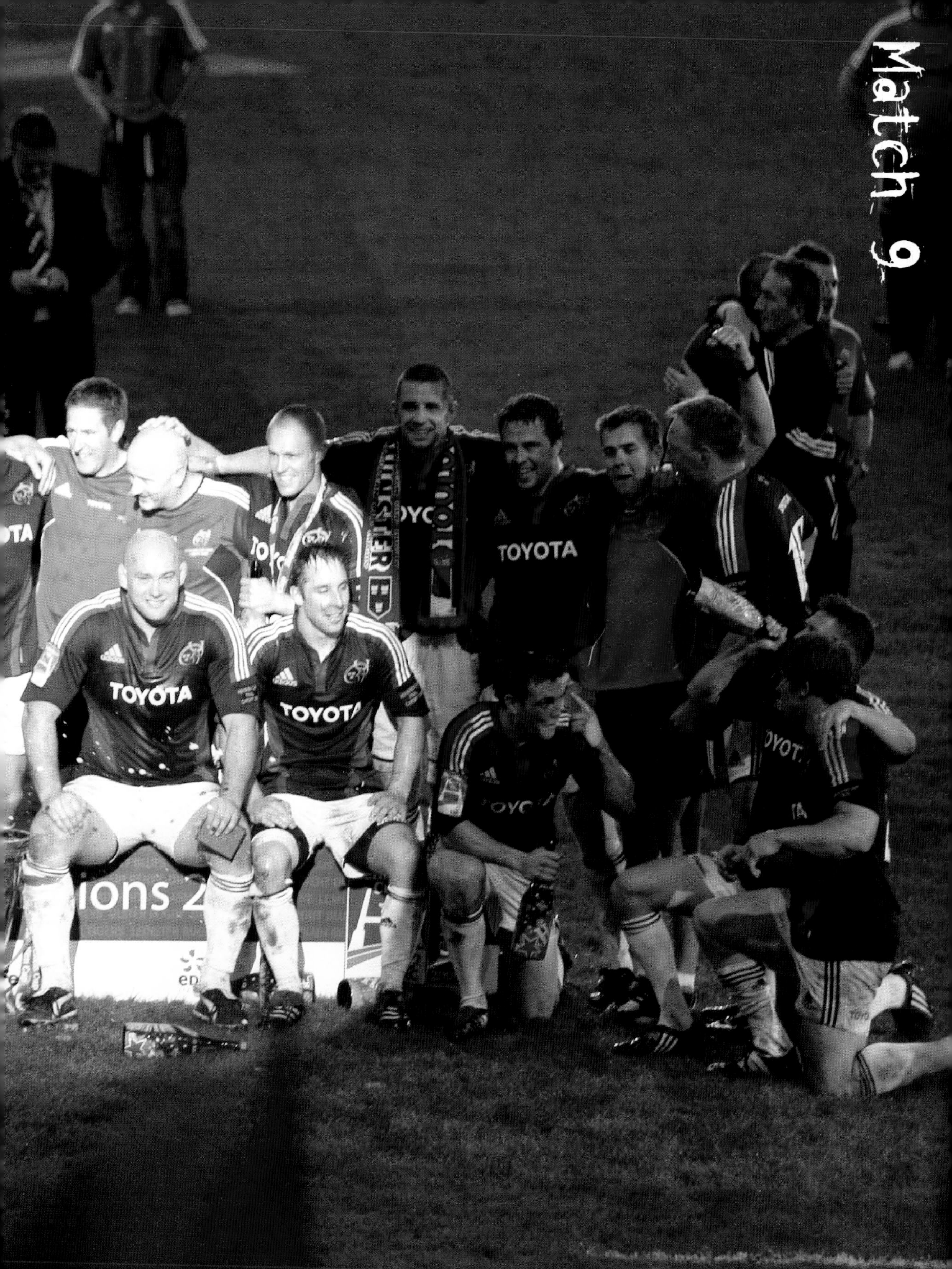

Proud father

Alan Quinlan celebrates with his
winners medal

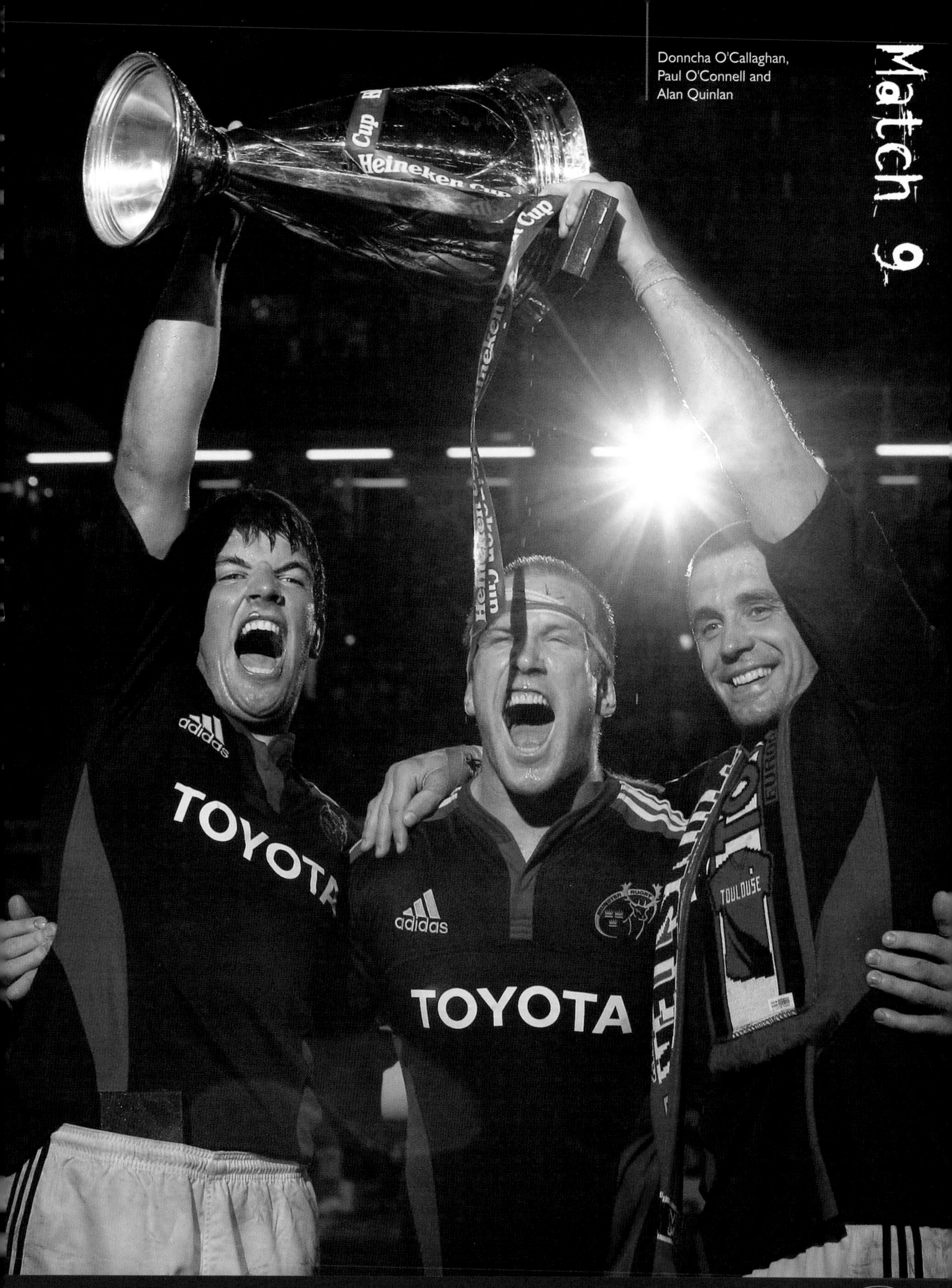

Donncha O'Callaghan,
Paul O'Connell and
Alan Quinlan

Kidney and O'Connell raise
the cup

Celebration on the victory podium

Howlett waves to the crowd

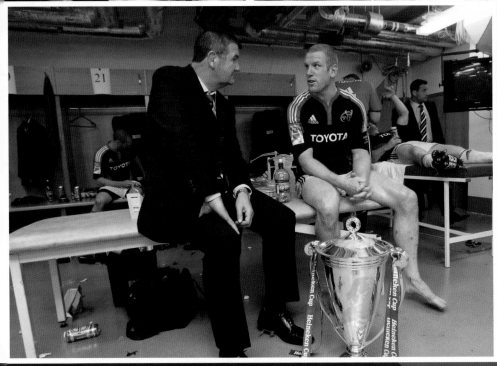

Anthony Foley and Mick O'Driscoll present the cup to the Limerick crowds

New Zealand trio, Doug Howlett, Rua Tipoki
and Lifeimi Mafi perform the Haka

Declan Kidney thanks fans for their support over the years

The Homecoming

The crowd shows their support in Cork

Kidney takes his final bow